Write a Screenplay

Written by: C.H. Da

Disclaimer

The information contained in this eBook, and its several complementary guides, is meant to serve as a comprehensive collection. Summaries, strategies, tips and tricks are only recommendations by the authors, and reading this eBook does not guarantee that one's results will exactly mirror our own results. The authors of this book have made all reasonable efforts to provide current and accurate information for the readers of this eBook. The authors will not be held liable for any unintentional errors or omissions that may be found.

Table of Contents

Introduction

Do you want to be a screenwriter?

Right now, you're probably screaming "Of course I do! Why else would I be reading this?" Congratulations! You are about to get a huge advantage on the competition.

Take a brief moment to ponder on all those screenwriters who you admire: Spielberg, Stone, Kaufman, and the others. None of them had a book like this to help them get started. They did it the old fashioned way – through trial and error. Sure, they had some brilliant ideas and a few connections but they did not have a blueprint to connect the dots between the various steps of writing a screenplay. That's one advantage that you do have. You're holding it in your hands at this very moment!

If that doesn't motivate you to start writing your screenplay, then I don't know what will. So sit down and get to writing. Good luck!

Just kidding! You bought this book for a reason. It's one thing to learn how to write a screenplay, but quite another to actually sit down behind a keyboard and write it. That's what makes this book so unique. I deliver the information in a way that will motivate you, helping you through the entire writing process. You will be instructed in a unique, reassuring way. And yes, I will give you a proverbial kick in the butt from time-to-time!

The foundation of a successful writing career is to actually write!

Sounds obvious, right?

The truth is not quite so clear cut. Most people who sit down to read books like this really do have every intention of following through. Unfortunately, most will then procrastinate and never go a damn thing!

99% of those who sit down to write a screenplay do not finish. 99%! Seems unreal, doesn't it? That leaves only 1% who will actually sit down and write their screenplay to completion.

In many ways, simply writing a screenplay is a huge achievement. It doesn't matter to some if they ever sell it. These people have fought past the mental block that kills 99% of aspiring writers before they can ever get started! This simple change in their mindset is priceless.

Putting together an entire screenplay is not an easy task and I will not lie and say that it is. That's why those who achieve their first screenplay have really accomplished a life changing goal. Holding their screenplay in their hands serves as proof that *it can be done.*

Now you have no excuse to not get started right now. Within 60 days you could be looking at your own screenplay and realizing its life-changing power. That's the purpose of this book – not just learning how it's done but to actually sit down and do it!

You can write a screenplay every 60 days. That's six screenplays in a year!

The first is always the toughest so once you get that one done, the rest will come much easier. There is no better educational experience for a writer (both new and experienced) than to plan, tackle, and complete a new writing project. The more you write, the easier it gets.

Now I want you to get a sheet of paper and write a contract for yourself. It should look something like this:

Insert Current Date

By (insert date 2 months from now) I will have written a complete screenplay. By accomplishing this monumental task, I will prove that I have the talent and ability to be a writer.

Sign it and date again.

This might seem a bit eccentric to some people but having a contract is essential. They are a normal part of the business so you should make one for yourself, sign it, and post it so that you are forced to look at it every single day. A contract will hold you accountable.

Rule 1: Writer's write!

If you truly want to become a screenwriter, then write a screenplay.

1

A Screenwriter's Life

Fame and fortune seem to be everyone in Hollywood's dream whether they are a model, actor, or even a writer. Some people get a lifetime of fame while others see their 15 minutes in a flash. Some examples of these short-lived experiences are reality stars whose faces are plastered all around magazine stands and then just a month later are seen being turned away from VIP access in the most popular clubs.

Becoming a big time Hollywood screenwriter is something that many are trying to do so there is a lot of competition. It's said that just about everyone in Hollywood has a screenplay tucked away on their computer and this is not an over-exaggeration. It's a fact. The industry is extremely tough and the competition is fierce.

This fact tends to scare many potential writers away from ever trying. The odds are stacked against you. So how can you ever hope to beat these kinds of odds? Hopefully your answer is this:

'I have to write! My stories must be told!'

Just as singers have to sing and painters have to paint, you should feel that you have to write. Writing must be your dream – not a way to become famous.

Why Become a Writer?

Hopefully, your answer matches the one above. There are much less competitive opportunities out there for those who simply want to become a writer. Journalism, blogging, and even writing novels are wonderful opportunities that have much less competition than screenwriting. We are a special breed, born with the obsession that our story needs to be seen. We use fame and fortune to mold others, not just ourselves. We imagine powerful characters and breathe life into them. Our ultimate goal is to form a connection with millions of viewers around the world.

A Screenwriter's Life

A screenwriter loves life, movies, and people. The whole *'I don't like other people'* mantra is not going to get you very far in this business. Trust me, I hear this from a lot of writers and I know instantly that they are not going to get very far.

A screenwriter doesn't just watch a movie, they climb inside of the screen. They pay attention to details, techniques, and characterization. They enjoy indie films and love to watch behind the scenes specials.

Screenwriters are definitely a special breed and they all have a story to tell; in fact, most have a lot of stories to tell. The difference between novelists and screenwriters is that screenwriters like to take full control while novelists let a reader's imagination do a lot of the work. Each requires a different mindset but I recommend that you look at both sides of the equation.

Bringing a story to life for producers, directors, and actors is the screenwriter's job. These are the ones who will ultimately take a screenplay and portray it for viewers. So as a screenwriter, you need to inspire these people.

Screenwriters are rarely celebrities but they are surrounded by the same fame and fortune. They get invited to all the cool parties. They are loved by a lot of the famous actors. Actors and directors might get the highest amount of fame, but the screenwriter is the one who ultimately creates it.

Most importantly, a screenwriter is doing what they love: telling a great story.

Who Can Become a Screenwriter?

There are three key elements to every screenwriter.

The first and perhaps most important element is that you must love movies. Great movies will give you goosebumps and stick in your mind for a long time after watching it. A horrible movie will cause you to shutter as if fingernails were being raked across a chalkboard. If you're one of those who prefer reading a novel over watching a good movie, then you should probably become a novelist.

Second is that you love to write. Sounds obvious, right?

Well it's amazing at how many people only try to write a screenplay to become famous. Writers have a gaping hole in them that is not filled by anything other than writing. Let me ask you two questions:

- When things are not going your way, do you feel better if you sit down and write about them?
- When things are great, do you write about that as well?

Even though you probably haven't tried writing a screenplay yet, you have tried your hand at writing short stories or maybe even keep a journal. If you have this gaping hole that is only filled by writing, then you are passionate about it!

Finally, the third factor is that you have a deep-seeded need to tell your story. Your main goal cannot be to become famous. It has to be that you truly want to tell your story. Look, if you write a great screenplay and are passionate about having your story heard, then all of that other stuff will happen. However, if you only care about fame and fortune then Hollywood executives will pick up on this.

It takes thick skin to break into the industry. You will need to persevere through a ton of adversity. You're guaranteed to get more rejections than signings. That should not stop you though so long as you are doing something that you absolutely love. Learn from each rejection to relieve the sting a bit.

"If you want to increase your success rate, double your failure rate."

~ Thomas J. Watson

Next time you watch the Academy Awards, pay attention to the age of screenwriters. You will notice that most are in their upper forties. That should tell you that it takes time to find success.

Every smart writer understands that Hollywood is tough. They keep writing anyway because they understand that writing is what writers do. I'm willing to put money on the odds that you will get rejected multiple times before you ever receive a positive letter. Rejection is normal. What separates success from failure is how you handle this rejection. Will you let it forge doubt into your heart or will you learn from each experience? I hope you choose the latter because if you let rejection control you, then you'll eventually give up.

On the other hand, if you learn to look at rejection as just another step up the ladder to success, you will be able to not only withstand rejection, but it will actually help you grow as a writer. For now, remember that writing your first screenplay is a huge achievement in itself. So if you have a completed screenplay within 60 days, then you are allowed to celebrate. You just made it further than 99% of aspiring writers!

Before you read any further, you should write down some questions and answer them. In fact, I recommend that you write these down and post them with your contract so that you are forced to look at them every day. Better yet, frame them.

- Why do you want to become a screenwriter instead of a novelist?
- What makes you want to share your story on the big screen?
- Name at least one thing that you feel is holding

you back from your dream of screenwriting?

- What motivates you the most?
- How will you handle rejection?
- How do you plan to market yourself in this industry?
- Are you willing to make sacrifices in order to see this through? List these sacrifices.
- Are there people in your life who will support and encourage you?
- List the real reasons that you want to become a screenwriter.

These will serve as your inspirational goals. Frame them and post them on your wall so that you see them on a daily basis.

Setting goals is a huge step in achieving any dream – this is not limited to screenwriting. After all, you can't take a trip without planning it. At least, I hope you would not try that. Telling yourself *"I hope to be a screenwriter one day so why not try"* is just not good enough.

When is one day?

"Do or do not; there is no try."

~**Yoda** *(Star Wars: The Empire Strikes Back)*

You won't get anywhere without listing attainable goals so it is vital to establish a list of goals right now.

Exercise 1A: Set your Goals

It's always a great idea to set high goals in the beginning but it's equally important to set realistic goals for how you plan to achieve these larger goals. Your first goal should be to create a deadline for finishing the first draft of your screenplay. Set an exact date! Then after that goal, set a second goal for what you will do once you achieve your deadline. When do you want to have your screenplay edited by?

Then comes your marketing goals, which should be planned out right now. How many agents and contests will you submit your screenplay to? Set a goal for creating a deadline and list.

Once you finish writing your screenplay, you can take a moment to celebrate but don't wait too long before you start sending out your screenplay. Once you do, take a week off and then start working on your next screenplay. Remember, writers write. We don't finish one screenplay and then stop writing. Try and complete as many screenplays as you can. Six screenplays per year is a good goal.

These screenplays are probably going to get rejected hundreds of times. Eventually an agent will bite so keep yourself motivated until they do. Read rejection letters and see if there is anything you can improve on your end.

All experienced screenwriters have a drawer full of screenplays that seemed great at the time but are now painful to read. These screenplays were not a waste of time. They were part of our development. In fact, these same screenplays can be crafted into a masterpiece later down the line. For now, you should write, send out query letters, and enter contests. You will continue to develop your skills but only if you keep writing.

Now I want you to sit down and set your goals for next month, six months, and one year from now. The first two months have pretty much been planned – to complete your first screenplay. Even if you think it's bad, just get the darn thing written.

After achieving that huge step, take a week off before you edit it. Your mind needs to be refreshed from time-to-time. We will discuss this in more detail later in this book. You might even rewrite some of your goals later. But for now, I want you to have a plan in place.

A great and manageable goal for beginners is to sit down and write no less than three complete and marketable screenplays in your first year. Slowly work up to a goal of completing six a year.

Over time, you will have dozens of screenplays in circulation which greatly increases your discoverability. Agents will start to recognize your name. Your skills will be improving too. Agents do take notice of writers who continuously improve their skills.

Setting goals is essential. If you're not planning to follow this advice then you are setting yourself up for a much tougher time and significantly decreasing your chances of success in screenwriting.

How to Write a Screenplay in 60 Days

You might think that this is just a far-fetched fantasy and that the only screenplays that are written in 60 days will be low quality. Writing a great screenplay in 60 days is completely possible. Consider these people.

- Mary Faulkner holds the Guinness World Record for writing the most books in a lifetime – completing 900 books.
- Novelist Georges Simenon wrote about 60 pages per day.
- Sylvester Stallone wrote Rocky in 3 days.
- William Shakespeare has had his works adapted for the big screen more than 300 times!

My point is that writing a screenplay in 60 days is a very realistic goal. This book will show you how to accomplish this without sacrificing quality. I'm going to show you how to:

- Develop your storytelling skills
- Transform your idea into a reality
- Format your screenplay like a professional
- Stay motivated throughout the entire process
- Edit and rewrite your screenplay (very important!)
- Sell your script
- Pitch your script

This book contains plenty of tips that will help you write your 60-day screenplay. Using exercises after each sections helps to make following this advice easier.

I'm not going to tell you what you want to hear the entire time. There will be times when I tell you what you need to hear. Writing can be stressful and will have you pulling your hair out sometimes. There are easy tips that I will discuss that will help avoid writer's block. Keep an open mind and I will help you through some of these tough moments.

Sign a Contract

Have you done this yet? If not, stop reading now and do it!

A contract binds you to a specific obligation and you should never break one. So if you really want to write a screenplay then commit to it by signing a contract. Make the commitment now! Again, this contract should include the time you signed it, as well as the time you plan to have your screenplay finished. Keep it short, simple and specific.

Prove that you are serious by signing that contract!

2

Becoming a Screenwriter

It's important for inspiring screenwriters to immerse themselves in the industry as deeply as possible. Watch plenty of movies. Compare the good against the bad so that you can see what makes great movies tick. When watching movies with friends or a significant other, gauge their reactions. Talk to them afterwards and ask them what they liked or disliked about it.

Make sure that you include artful movies, as well as movies from all genres. Don't limit yourself to being an expert within a single genre. You may not have any interest in certain niches but you can still apply some of them into other genres to add more substance to your screenplay.

Pay careful attention to the style used in the movie you watch. Over time, you will begin to train your *'eye'* to see how movies are put together and notice elements that a casual viewer might miss. Hooks, camera angles, and killer dialogue are just a few of the elements.

Be aware of how the movie is structured. The structure of a movie is the way it sets up. For example, how does a specific situation cause a character to react? How does the overall plot cause the protagonist to transform?

Watching a movie from the screenwriter's perspective means that you ask yourself:

- How was the film structured? Was it understandable? Did it make sense? Could you follow how one event led to the next? Was the overall plot too obvious or too subtle?
- What makes the movie work? Plot? Storyline? Characters? Dialogue?
- Did the tension build at an acceptable pace or was the movie boring? Lack of tension will ultimately lead you to stop watching a movie. If this is the case, at what point did it become unbearable?

Screenwriting

There are several different styles of screenwriting but the most common are for feature films and television scripts. Other types of screenwriting include:

- Documentaries
- Multimedia
- Musicals
- Television Drama
- Situational Comedies
- Talk or News Shows
- Shorts
- Stage plays

Becoming a screenwriter isn't as complicated as many tend to believe. So long as you write then everything else will fall into place. There is a formula that most successful screenwriters use.

The Screenwriting Formula

This formula consists of five easy steps.

Inspiration is the best friend to any writer. Watching movies and reading novels should inspire you. Learn how to spot what works for other writers and turn these powers into your own. Don't be afraid to imitate another writer. You don't have to reinvent the wheel. You only need to craft your screenplay into a unique story. Using styles that are already established is perfectly fine.

Watch films and television within the same genre as you plan to write in. A screenwriter doesn't normally watch movies just to be entertained. They pay attention to every aspect of them – from camera angles to characters. A screenwriter will notice things that the normal viewer does not even consider.

Reading is another critical aspect of any writer – including screenwriters. Novels provide visual references through words whereas a screenplay provides visual effects. Your job is to serve as a bridge between the two, giving just enough description for the director to transform it into a scene. Furthermore, novels serve as great tools for grasping a feel for dialogue, descriptions of people, and scene changes.

Dedicate the time to become successful. Even if you are working a full time job, you still need to find the time to write. Most writers lead a hectic lifestyle. This is even truer for writers trying to get discovered since they still have to pay the bills! What separates successful writers from dreamers is that they make the time to write. You can write for just one hour a day and still meet the overall goal of a screenplay every 60 days. I'm confident that you can find a way to fit one hour of writing into your daily routine. Maybe wake up an hour earlier or even go to bed an hour later? Define your own motivation for writing, then get in front of a keyboard and do it!

Exercise. A healthy body leads to a healthy mind. Be sure to schedule in some time to exercise. You'll be amazed at how wonderful exercising will make you feel.

Also, you should exercise your writing skills. Just like an athlete stretches before the big game, you should find your rhythm as a writer before tackling that next scene.

Some Good Writing Exercises

- Find your favorite scene of your favorite movie and then try changing it. Rewrite the scene through your own eyes. Once you are done *"stretching,"* dive directly into your screenplay.
- Choose your favorite character from any film you want and write their biography.
- Choose any of your characters and then write a secret that they do not want anyone else in the story to know. It can be anything you want.

Following these five simple guidelines will keep you on the right track. Remember that working hard is not what will make you successful – working smart is the true key to unlocking success. So following a path will help you tremendously.

How to Find Inspiration

In the previous section, I explained that inspiration is a key component for writers. There are many different ways that you can find inspiration. You can watch movies, play games, or even visit a coffee house. Music can be a huge inspiration to some while bothersome to others. Taking long walks can combine exercising with inspiration. The key is to find what fuels your fire. What inspires you the most?

"1. The act or power of moving the intellect or emotions.
2. The quality or state of being inspired."

~Merriam-Webster Dictionary

The most important question you need to answer is this.

What does it take for you to feel inspired?

Normally for writers, anything that drags you out of your daily routine will serve as inspiration. As a screenwriter, you need to be aware of your environment at all times. Doing so will reveal your inspirations.

Keep a journal!

You heard me. A journal is very important to a writer so if you want constant inspiration then you should keep a journal. It also gives you a place to write short stories, take note of people's behavior, and even put your own emotions into writing. All of this will help you add depth to everything you write.

Having a notebook handy when you're inspired gives you a place to write down these thoughts, ideas, or maybe even a cool catch phrase you might have overheard!

Always carry a notebook with you wherever you go!

Do not waste real life opportunities simply because you don't have a notebook with you when inspiration hits. If you try to remember something, you're going to forget it. You will have missed a huge opportunity. You have to write it down!

Exercise 2: Become a Film Critic

As you become more experienced in the art of screenwriting, you're going to find yourself being inspired by anything you watch on television. You're going to naturally be critical of everything you watch from this moment forward. So take it a step further by writing it down.

1. What made the movie/show good?

Or

2. What made the movie/show bad?

Creating lists such as this will help you subconsciously determine what type of screenplay you want to write. Create as many entries as you can and add more as you expand your experience.

Read through this list on a weekly basis so that these pros and cons soak into your mind.

Develop a Camera Eye

As mentioned earlier, a screenwriter must always be

aware of their environment. Develop a three-dimensional concept of everything around you. For example, most people cast their eyes upon a lake and see blue water or maybe a tan boat gliding across it. On the other hand, a screenwriter will gaze upon the same sight and see the boat gliding across the calm waters as the sunlight bounces harmlessly off its surface. A screenwriter will hear the whistling of a bird perched on the drooping branch in the background. A dog barks in the distance echoing its howl across the calm waters. A screenwriter will smell the fresh breeze as it gently grazes their face. Do you see my point?

A screenwriter doesn't just witness a scene. They become immersed in it. They use all of their senses to experience it. Screenwriters see colors and light in more detail. Next time you are standing outside, ask yourself the following question:

How would I describe this in a scene?

Now that's not saying that a screenwriter should be as detailed as I was above. We are simply observant of these things. We have to create these senses by using as few words as possible. That is the challenge of screenwriting and is what's known as a *"camera eye"*.

A screenwriter should always view the world in scenes, sounds, colors, dialogue, and lighting. Turn on your imagination on a daily basis. Transform the real world into a fantasy. Revive the child inside – that child who was so imaginative. Without this imaginative approach, your screenplay will be flat and dull.

Learn to Develop your Senses

Let's start by developing your other senses. Put on a blindfold for a few minutes each day and pay attention to what all of your other senses are telling you. When done, write it all down in your journal. Describe what you heard, felt, smelled, or even tasted during that time. Be as detailed as possible.

When you first start out, you might find it difficult to be detailed. That's okay. Just keep getting more detailed each time and before you know it, you'll be taking note of the way your heart raced when you heard that kid down the hall screaming bloody murder!

Sight is the easiest sense to articulate. A screenwriter needs to learn to hone the rest of their senses.

Another good exercise is to find a random object in your home. Write a paragraph that describes it. Then go back and rewrite that description the next day, improving upon it. Keep doing this on a daily basis until you are evoking as much description as possible.

Then take that same description and shave down the word count. Evoke as much description but with fewer words. This is an important skill to develop as a screenwriter.

Now go even further by taking out as many adjectives as possible. You will soon get the hang of it. Once you do, you will have developed a very important skill.

3

Become a Storyteller

First of all, let me reveal a fact that is not exactly common knowledge. The most common response a writer gets when they tell a stranger that they are a writer is “People always tell me that I should write a book.” Why do you think that is?

Everyone has a story to tell.

Not only that, but most of these stories deserve to be told. However, 99% of these people will never tell their stories. So stop asking yourself if you have a story to tell because you do. Instead, start asking yourself if you have the courage to tell it.

Before we go any further, I want you to define why you need to tell your story. If your goal is to get rich, then you probably shouldn’t waste your time.

Good reasons for writing are:

- To inspire others
- To educate others by sharing your experience
- Provide hope to others
- Entertain others

These are all the reasons why writers choose this profession. We need to accomplish one of these goals. Without true motivation outside of financial concerns, a writer will have trouble keeping it real. Screenwriters who enter this business with aspirations of getting rich are usually disappointed.

Throw that concept out of the window right now!

Great screenplays are believable. Writers can only be believable when they truly believe in what they are writing. Does that make sense?

Now that I've went through reasons to become a writer, let's talk about how to become a storyteller (you know, the topic that this chapter is devoted to).

Write from the heart!

This doesn't mean that everything you write needs to be based on your life story. Everything you write is not going to be an exact replica of your life. You just need to be sure that you take pieces from your life and incorporate them into your story. Simply write about things you know to make it more believable.

Remember that you should be keeping a notebook. Use it to draw ideas from these real experiences to make your screenplay more believable. The only alternative is that you manufacture these scenarios from scratch. That's a bad idea. Screenplays that are manufactured like this are going to fall flat.

You should be exaggerating real life experiences.

Everyone is unique and it's these unique perspectives that make a screenplay really pop. Do you think that your life is boring? Guess what? There is no such thing as a boring life! As a member of society, you were born unique, you live a unique life, and you will die unique.

Let's use your hometown as an example. If you were raised in a small town then someone who grew up in Los Angeles would find your perspective on life unique and interesting. Vise versa, someone growing up in a small town would find the big city life just as fascinating. My point is that you should be comfortable telling a story from your own perspective. There's no need to manufacture anything at all. Never try to be anyone other than yourself. Any story can be transformed from dull to interesting by infusing it with regular injections of real life.

Creativity and honesty go hand-in-hand. Don't be afraid to embellish.

Fiction is simply taking believable characters, throwing them into a believable situation, and then letting your imagination fill in the gaps. Your goal is to make viewers care about what happens to these characters. They will care because these characters could be real people – they are real in a sense. For them to come across as real, these characters will need to be based on experiences that are also real.

Research is another way that you can create real characters in real events. If you want to write a detective screenplay but don't have any experience in this field, then you will need to research it. This is perfectly okay but it's not recommended for those new to screenwriting. New screenwriters should write what they know.

Your characters should be forged from the behaviors, traits, and challenges of people you personally know. Don't be afraid to mix and match. If you have one friend who is goofy and another who is extremely shy, then you might combine them to create a character that is awkward in situations with a lot of people.

Let your imagination run wild. Research in order to give your story an edge but never let it distract you from telling your story. Don't spend days working out a single scene. Just write. You will be editing later.

Researching

This is yet another reason why you're keeping a journal. Take notes and always have a running list of questions and/or topics in your journal.

When writing your screenplay, always write about things you know first. If you happen to come across something that needs research, then highlight it and move on. Do not stop writing in order to research. Once you have written most of the draft, then you can go back to those highlighted areas.

Here are some of the best methods for researching:

- Online
- Interviewing someone who is experienced in the area you need to research
- Send out emails to several experts
- Encyclopedia

The Art of Storytelling

According to Aristotle, every successful story was comprised of three "acts". These acts keep it interesting and most importantly, keep people's attention. Let's look at the three acts of a story.

Act 1: The Set-Up

This act teases the audience much like the words "once upon a time" that are used in fairy tales. The set-up must have a hook – something that makes the audience want to keep reading/watching. In terms of a screenplay, this should happen within the first five to ten pages.

The set-up also builds up to Act 2.

Act 2: The Conflict

Without conflict, there would be no story. Well to be more precise, there would be no reason to tell the story. Have you ever watched a movie with a huge build up only to find out that nothing really happened? It's those kinds of movies that might make you mumble, "There's 2 hours of my life that I'm never getting back."

This scenario is the result of a lack of conflict. I can never make it through these types of movies and always end up walking out. Without conflict, what's the point?

Act 3: The Resolution

Once you have built up enough conflict, it's time to resolve it. There's nothing that frustrates a viewer more than to discover that they followed a character for over an hour for nothing! It's important to remember that while not all stories have a happy ending, all stories must have a resolution. Your character should change as a result of their experiences throughout the story.

Sequences

Although a screenplay revolves around a central plot, there are always scenes that are separate, yet tied together by the central plot. These are known as sequences. Just like with the overall plot, these are comprised of a beginning, middle, and end. A sequence can be seen as a story within the main story.

Sequences Exercise

Think of your favorite movie and consider what the overall plot was based on. Now look for sequences within that plot. Write them in your journal as practice. Take note of where each sequence begins and ends while also observing the conflict of each sequence.

Determine What to Write

Do you have a brilliant story to tell but are waiting for the perfect time to tell it? Maybe it's your life story but you feel that you're not old enough to articulate it at this point in your life.

Stop waiting! There is no better time to tell your story than now.

The best move you can make for your writing career is to write your story now. Waiting is what leads so many to never tell their stories. Tell the story that you are excited about – that story that you close your eyes and see as clearly as your own life. That's what you should be writing and you should be writing it now. Don't be afraid. Fear will only lead to doubt and it will ultimately lead to regret. This regret will haunt you forever.

As writers, we are often inspired by certain things. These passions change and evolve as we gain new experiences. That's why it's so important that you work towards what inspires you now because it might not always be a part of who you are. A fear of tackling these inspirations leads so many writers to failure because they are preventing themselves from gaining the lessons needed to tell the next story. They make no progress and eventually give up.

Face your fears and start telling your story today!

How to Get Started Writing

Explore your backstory. It's key to write down the events that lead up to your story. These are events that take place before the first page. Write as many pages as you can about your characters' lives. Your goal is to set up your characters, settings, and events that will eventually lead to your story. This not only makes writing easier but it will enrich your story.

Write journals for your characters. You read that correctly. Take the time to put yourself into the shoes of your characters and write a journal from their perspective. The goal is to create enough of a backstory so that characters will essentially write themselves. This is not an exaggeration. Ask any successful screenwriter or novelist and they will all tell you that characters take on a life of their own. So sit down and fill out a journal for your characters. Detail the pains and joys of their life. It will help you understand what they are fighting for. They will start making decisions that surprise you. Every one of us has essences that define our lives. They take part in every decision we make. Don't try and do this in your head. Write it down!

Raise the stakes before you write a single page of your screenplay. Writers mistakenly try and tell a story completely truthfully – every aspect of it. So before you start writing, you should heighten the tension. Make the needs of each character dynamic so that the story does not seem boring. People who are placed into highly intense situations will often make the most unpredictable choices. This is what makes a great story so compelling.

Telling a story is not an easy task. It puts a lot of demand on a writer's heart and soul. Never be half-assed about it. Be bold and take the time to do it right!

4

Developing your Story

Now that you understand what makes a great story compelling, it's time to develop your story. The first aspect is the genre.

Genre

Let's get to it! The first is the most basic. Who is your target audience? What is your genre? Popular genres include:

- Romance
- Comedy
- Drama
- Action
- Mystery
- Fantasy
- Science Fiction

Developing your Story

Now let's look at some more technical aspects of your story to determine the audience. Ask yourself these questions:

- When is the story set? (Past, Present, or Future)
- Where is it set?
- What is the story's tone? (Tragedy, Surreal, Dramatic, Slapstick)
- Which character's point of view will the story be told from?
- Will the story be narrated?
- Will it include flashbacks?

Most books will recommend that you have a plan for telling your story before you start writing. I'm going to contradict this a little bit. So long as you have followed this book so far, you can sit down now and start writing. See where your imagination leads you. Do whatever feels right.

I'm willing to bet that you already have a story in head and that you have your main characters already laid out. So just start writing. Don't over-think it. Don't worry too much about grammar and typos. I know writers who constantly worry about finding the perfect words for every single sentence before moving onto the next. These are the same people who have been trying to write their story for years to no avail. Finding the perfect words is part of editing, which comes later but you need a draft to work with. So just write!

If you keep writing, events will start to unfold. Ideas will come out of nowhere! Your entire story could change and that's okay. This happens because your characters are likely to surprise you. They have a say in how your story turns out. Your characters will help you tell the story so all you have to do is write it down.

When you get to the point where your characters are essentially telling the story for you, it's known as the writing zone. It's when we write our best works. It's only achieved through a high understanding of our characters and by viewing them as real people. They have the same flaws and traits as every single one of us. By writing (not thinking, just writing) you will get their stories down on paper for the world to see.

That's why backstory is so important. It helps you get into the writing zone. They become your best friends. So if you do the work of creating as much backstory as possible, you will never have to guess what your characters will do in a given situation. They will tell you!

Don't take my word for this. Read interviews of other writers. Listen to how they refer to characters in their stories. They refer to them in the third-person.

Tapping into your characters makes your job extremely easy. Listening and writing will be your only tasks. There will be no need to over-think anything.

Creating Notes

Screenwriting programs all have a feature for keeping notes that relate to your plot, subplot, theme, characters, and settings. This is a powerful feature and you should use it to your fullest advantage. It gives you easy access to information on an as needed basis. Since you will need to be consistent with names, places, and ages, utilizing this feature will make your job much easier. These small details can make or break a screenplay. Trust me, viewers will notice if you make a mistake. Instead of wasting time by sorting through your draft, wouldn't it be better to have this information readily available?

Let's use one of your characters as an example. You will need to create a profile that consists of:

- Age
- Career
- Friends
- Family
- Hobbies
- Where they live

Then you can move onto more detailed topics like:

- Experience with addiction (most people at least know someone who has struggled with an addiction of some kind)
- Sexual experience (religious context, successes, failures)
- Political viewpoints

- Religious viewpoints
- Abandonment issues (more common than you might think)
- Love life
- What makes them angry?
- What makes them happy?
- What are their fears?
- Are they optimistic or pessimistic? Also explain why.

Never stop asking questions about your characters. Imagine you are interviewing him/her and ask the same questions.

Their voice is important! Do they have an accent? Do they gesture when they speak?

Ask the questions and be sure that you write the answers down. Start out with generic questions and then move onto more specific ones. Eventually, you will wonder how in the heck you created such a realistic character.

Character Development

Developing characters is the key to creating a successful screenplay. I've hit you over the head repeatedly with that statement. It's that important. So now let's take a look at some successful techniques for developing your main characters into award winning roles.

As I've already mentioned, backstory is extremely important. I've even discussed interviewing them in order to create that backstory. So now let's take that strategy a step further by asking them even more specific questions.

1. Who are the most important people in that character's life? It could be their lover, spouse, parent, or even a best friend. Heck, it could be their pet. Some characters love themselves more than anything else – at least in the beginning. You also need to know what kind of bond they have with this person/pet. What kind of relationship is it?

2. What is your character's profession? Does he/she love to work with numbers? Maybe they are great with numbers but hate that sort of work? Establishing their career will give them traits and/or weaknesses to work with.

3. What kind of personality does this character have? Is he laid back or high strung? Most people are either one or the other. What triggers his most extreme reactions? What sets his off? What are his fears and pet peeves?

4. What are your character's motivations? What makes him tick? By establishing hi overall motivations, you will be better able to push him to the extreme.

5. What is his/her family history? This is often a defining trait for all people. It establishes how a person is and can be a catalyst for fears and/or other important traits.

Although it's definitely important to develop a backstory, it's equally important to give your characters real qualities that others can relate to. You make them more believable and it creates a much more entertaining environment for your audience. They will care what happens to these characters.

Here are even more specific questions that you should ask your characters:

- What is his favorite music?
- What is his greatest secret?
- Does he read? If so, what's his favorite book?
- Does he love sports or despise them?
- What kind of car does he drive?
- What is his obsession?
- Does he dream of being wealthy?
- Who is your character's influence? Why? How do they relate?
- Does your character have an uninspired nickname?
- Does your character have any annoying habits?

Your goal is to transform a good character into a great one by humanizing them. Play around with their human nature and don't be afraid to give them a totally unique personality.

Just like people in your real life, you might often find contrasting characteristics in your characters. So try to give every character at least one of these.

By injecting real humanity into your characters, you will have already provided your audience with valuable insight. Real people are always unique. They have contrasting behaviors and contradictory moods. It's what makes each of us unique. Texture your characters with these real traits and stay true to them. They will become the rule that your universe must follow.

Common Character Types

Your characters are the most important aspect of your screenplay. You could have the perfect plot laid out but without characters that your audience can connect with, they won't care about your story's plot.

The Hero

Inspire your audience through your main character. More often than not, your main character is the hero (or heroine). This is not always true but in most cases it is. No matter what type of hero you decide to create, this character must be likable. The audience must want them to win. They must also be placed in a losing battle or scenario in order to make them even more lovable. Your audience will then root for them to overcome these insurmountable odds and emerge victorious.

The main character is known in writing terms as the **protagonist**. This is the character that an audience can identify with.

An **alter-ego** character is one that resembles the writer. Most of the greats often include one of these in each story they tell. The idea is to use personal beliefs, thoughts, and experiences to get the point across. When developing an alter ego character you need to dive deep into your own psyche. Since you're not making this up, this is the one character that should come across as the most believable to your audience.

Now let's talk a little bit about **polar attitude**. This is your protagonist's approach to other characters or more precisely, their emotional attitude towards them. As your plot unfolds, the protagonist will encounter changes in their polar attitude. Your audience should always remain connected through these changes, even when the character is doing things that are morally wrong. The audience believes that their heart is in the right place.

By understanding your main character's motivations, you should start developing them right away. Lay out a plan on how you will accomplish this. How will a certain situation change your protagonist? Figure that out by answering these questions:

What is the character very headstrong about? What would change their mind about this? Will this change happen gradually or instantly?

How will a conflict affect his/her behavior? Will they become stronger, weaker, or more lovable? On the other hand, it might make them angry, resentful, and even flat out rude!

Does your character need to overcome some sort of emotional or physical handicap? If so, then how will they be able to overcome this huge obstacle?

Now let's look at the **catalytic character**. This is a character that encourages or even forces your protagonist to change. This type of character can easily be mistaken for the protagonist so it's important to be careful when creating him/her. Make use of them early and often. Aside from your protagonist, this is probably the most important character in a story.

Next we will move onto the **composite character**. Some writers choose not to use their own stories or beliefs with their protagonist so they develop a composite character. This character is often based on someone the writer knows (although you can never openly admit this). Explore the way they think, feel, and react in specific conflicts.

A Hero's Journey

This is the path that a protagonist takes to get from Act 1 to Act 3. There is no story without a journey of some kind. This journey can happen on an emotional level or physically – sometimes both. For now, let's explore the more literal sense of a hero's journey.

This journey was the basis for Star Wars. Luke Skywalker followed a path to get from Tatooine to the Death Star. This journey took place over 3 movies – all of which are perfect examples of the 3 distinct parts of the hero's journey.

Part 1: Departing

This is the hero's start to the journey. They either begin voluntarily or are forced down the path. This is also known as a "call to action". It provides the hero with an opportunity to gain something valuable (spiritually or physically) by facing the unknown. The hero might be trying to reclaim something that has been stolen, seeking revenge, or just finding that missing piece in their life.

By answering this call to action, the protagonist will cross over what is known as *"the threshold"*. At this point, the adventure really takes off. Your protagonist might meet a dark figure who blocks his path and he will not be able to proceed until he defeats this figure.

Example

Using *'Star Wars'* as an example, the movie *'A New Hope'* follows this part of the hero's journey. Luke Skywalker is thrust into the battle against the Empire in two ways. First, his Aunt and Uncle are killed (call to action). He meets his mentor who teaches him the ways of the Force (threshold). We know at the end of this movie that Luke Skywalker will have to eventually face Darth Vader in order to succeed.

Part 2: The Initiation

During this phase, the hero enters a strange world and faces strange forces that put him/her to the ultimate test. This consists of a series of challenges which are designed to exploit his/her weaknesses. In the end, the hero will face his/her greatest fear. At this point, they will face the dark figure for the first time.

The hero will fail here but transform as a result. This revelation changes the way they think and they are a different person as a result. The hero develops and gains a better understanding of himself. This entire process is known as “atonement”.

Example

You guessed it! *‘Star Wars: The Empire Strikes Back’* is the perfect example of this second part of a hero’s journey.

Luke Skywalker continues his journey, learning the ways of the *Force* from Yoda. The audience gains a better understanding of his own strengths and weaknesses. He is strong with the *Force* but cannot control it. However, when his close friends are taken captive by Darth Vader, he is forced into a confrontation.

Luke Skywalker loses the battle (and a hand). Furthermore, his deepest fears are realized upon revelation of Darth Vader being his father. This confrontation completely changes him.

Part 3: The Return

The initiation has changed the protagonist and now they return to their home or wherever they started the journey. They use their newfound traits to face and conquer the antagonist. The protagonist must face their deepest fears and overcome them. Finally, they have developed into their final stage.

Example

'Star Wars: Return of the Jedi' is perfectly named as *"the return"*. The movie starts as Luke returns to his home planet as a Jedi Knight to clean up the pieces shattered during his initiation. He then faces Darth Vader, who has also undergone his own character development (antagonists must also develop as characters). In fact, George Lucas effectively shifted the antagonist from Darth Vader to the Emperor. Luke's development changed his fears. While starting out as a fear of losing those closest to him, during the final confrontation,

Luke feared being turned to the Dark Side (since his father fell victim to this fate).

A hero's journey is a great formula for writing an effective story. It should also serve as a metaphor for your own life. You started out as a child and everything you did helped to develop you into who you are now. Guess what? You also went through the same stages as we discussed. Maybe not in a literal sense, but you emotionally followed the journey.

The Villain

As I mentioned in the previous section, a strong storyline requires a great villain. Some of the best movies I've seen and the best books I've read all had memorable villains. The antagonist must create obstacles that the protagonist must fight through. The idea is to make the protagonist's journey difficult.

Great antagonists scheme, plot, lie, and manipulate others in order to keep the hero from achieving their overall goals. This can be done directly or indirectly.

Establishing a backstory for the antagonist is just as important a task as it was for your protagonist. Use the same interview technique to do this. In many cases, the antagonist has experiences that led them down the path they are on now. He might have lost a lover or been abused as a child. Society might have ridiculed or even rejected him.

Watching news broadcasts and studying notorious criminals in real life are great methods for learning why villains do the things they do. Most people are not inherently evil – they simply perform evil deeds for a sense of adding self-value to their life. The truth is that there is a reason for every inherently evil act, some cases are just less obvious that others. As a writer, you should become a student of psychology.

Most of us have thought about revenge or righting wrongs done to us at some point in our lives. Dig these skeletons out of your closet and study them. Why did you have these kinds of thoughts? Explore what makes evil tick. Also, in the real world, the most evil minds like Hitler and Charles Manson were also extremely intelligent.

You must define your antagonist's motives. Their motives will be much stronger than the protagonist's at the beginning of your story. Your antagonist can be driven by any of the following:

Obsession: Generally, an obsession is centered around a love interest that both your protagonist and antagonist will share. It could be an ex-spouse or maybe even a high school crush that the antagonist cannot have.

Their past: An antagonist might have a past that continuously haunts them. Maybe your protagonist and antagonist are old high school rivals? The protagonist might have unknowingly hurt them in the past.

Greed: In many cases, the protagonist will possess something that the antagonist wants. It could be money or something priceless. It could even be that the protagonist was given something that the antagonist believes that they deserved.

Politics and/or Religion: Sometimes there is a war of ethical or moral beliefs between the main character and antagonist. Is the antagonist trying to change society's viewpoint in some huge political matter? There are even times when the antagonist is acting based on some religious belief.

Even if the audience never knows all of the reasons why the antagonist is motivated to do what they are doing, it's important that you (as the writer) know. These motivations will bring the character to life.

You will also need to establish what will happen to the antagonist in advance.

- Will he/she transform into a better person?
- Will the antagonist get away with their actions or will they be punished?
- Do you want the audience to hope for a change or hope for his/her head?

5

Developing Support Characters

Every story has supporting characters. They are used to enhance the story and serve a vital role in the protagonist's journey. They normally have a strong bond with the protagonist and are sometimes even the reason behind their actions to begin with.

A great supporting character will help the protagonist find his/her strengths and weaknesses. Sometimes they are traits that the protagonist never knew existed.

There are different types of supporting characters and each one has their own roles to play.

Let's start out with the **Archetypical character**. These characters are vulnerable and in desperate need of help. Children often assume this role but there are times when an elder or maybe even a lonely woman can assume it.

A mentor character serves as a guide to help the protagonist achieve his/her goals. They lead them in the right direction and teach them valuable skills. They impart wisdom. Mentors play an important role in developing storylines in certain plots.

Stock characters are generic and often show up several times throughout the course of a story. They have no real depth but are often set apart by a unique trait that stands out.

- The girl next door
- The prankster
- Femme-fatale
- Guy in the blue suit
- The mad scientist
- Womanizer
- Dumb Blonde

Support Characters Exercise

Think of your favorite movies and comprise a list of support characters from them. Try and find at least three of each type. Then describe how each support character affected the protagonist.

Character Interaction

Now that you have developed all of your characters (I know that was a lot of work), it's time that you start putting them together. Determine how they are going to interact with one another. This will be natural so long as you developed a detailed backstory.

- Shy characters will be passive around others.
- Outspoken characters will be very open.
- Obnoxious characters generally don't care what others think.
- Persistent characters normally know how to get what they want.
- Honest characters acknowledge their flaws and take ownership of them.

- Liars lie consistently.
- Heroic personalities fight for justice.
- Nervous characters will stutter, sweat, and even get nose bleeds when pulled out of their comfort zone.

The list is endless but I feel that you get the point. Once you have determined how your protagonist will act around specific people, you will be able to start writing your story. This interaction might change as the plot develops. However, if there is a change then it must happen gradually and the change must be justified.

Another way that characters interact is through witty repartee. This is a series of sarcastic comments based off of each character's previous line.

Dialogue is important but is not the end all and be all of character interaction. An audience will need more. Characters will behave a certain way in a give situation. They will also act differently in that same situation with another character than they do alone. Silent actions can be just as powerful as spoken words if done correctly.

Relationships between characters generally come with a theme. Here are some examples:

1. Beauty and the Beast: This is when an extremely attractive hero/heroine falls for a type of character who they might not normally be attracted to.

2. Opposites Attract: In this case, the two characters come from complete opposite cultures and have no understanding of each other's logic. Then they will learn to respect each other's views or can even fall in love in some cases.

3. Ugly becomes Beautiful: This type of theme is commonly found in romantic comedies and refers to the development of a character from the point when they were unappealing to their full development into an irresistible force.

4. A Common Goal: Characters from completely different walks of life join together to accomplish the same goal. During the journey, they find out that they have more in common than they might have thought.

Interaction Exercise

Visit your local coffee house, restaurant, the park, or even a local café. Observe how different people interact with each other. Once it's over, write the interactions down in your journal.

Do this once a week. Maybe you can treat yourself to breakfast or lunch once a week? Maybe you can include a walk through the park as part of your exercise routine? Whatever the case, you should observe interaction and take notes in your journal.

Determining How Many Characters to Include

This is one of the areas where screenplays and novels take off in different directions. Screenplays have limitations and characters are one of those limits. While a novel can include as many characters as the writer wants, there are factors that make it necessary to limit characters within a screenplay. When trying to break through, limit the number of characters to as few as possible.

Budget: As a screenwriter, you're going to have to worry about your screenplay's budget. While it doesn't cost you anything to write it, it will cost money to film it. The three leading factors in a screenplay's budget are casting, length, and special effects. The more characters that you include in your screenplay, the more talent will have to be cast. I wouldn't worry too much about this when writing your draft. You should just write. When editing, pull any unnecessary characters out of your screenplay.

Supporting Characters: Your protagonist needs support so you will have to include at least one supporting character in your screenplay: you can choose whether the mentor, catalytic, or archetypal works best for your screenplay. If your story needs it, then feel free to add more than one supporting character.

Character's Age: You will need to pay attention to your characters' ages. This is not really a budgeting issue. It's more of an issue to consider for your target audience. If you are targeting 20-30 year olds, then it's not likely they will watch a movie based on kids.

Creating Dynamic Characters

It takes discipline to create characters that are believable. Dynamic characters require that we don't impose our own beliefs and thoughts onto how they act. I won't lie; this is extremely difficult to master. However, a screenplay's characters are often the difference between successful scripts and ones that collect dust in the closet.

I have given you a great method of creating dynamic characters but you will need the discipline to follow it through. Following this process makes your characters more naturally dynamic. You must ask yourself whether you want to write a screenplay that the audience absolutely loves or one that they just find mildly entertaining.

The first step to creating more believable characters is to understand that dynamic characters are not magic. The equation is something like this:

Ta=D(Ti)

Talent = Discipline (Time)

Talent is not magic. It's a practice that takes a lot of dedication. The more you write, the better you will get. This includes your ability to create dynamic characters. I've laid out a system that will work so long as you follow it. I want you to focus more on writing and less on worrying about making your first screenplay perfect. Here are some more tips for creating dynamic characters.

1. Label the Character's Desires

Finding the major motivations in your character's life should always be the first thing you do. By generating backstory, you should be able to list these desires fairly easily. We all have personal motivations that drive every decision we make. They also show themselves in our actions and reactions to certain situations. These make each of us unique. So on your character notes, I want you to create a field called "Desires" and list these factors for easy reference.

2. Label the Character's Fears

What triggers your character's darkest side? Each desire listed in the previous step should have its own fear associated with it. These fears are going to battle your character's aspirations for achieving their desires. The two opposites will constantly be at war with each other for control of the character's actions. So labeling these fears will create imperfection within your character. Imperfection makes a character more dynamic.

3. Get Even More Specific with your Backstory

Human psychology consists of a chain of actions and reactions. At any given moment, our behavior is a battle between our goal and a fear that's associated with that goal. This directly impacts the choices we make. Fears and desires are usually based on past experiences. The whole process happens on a subconscious level. Experiences leave imprints on our very core, which is why no two people are the same. Dynamic characters are unaware that these past experiences are affecting their choices. Your audience will also be unaware.

However, as the writer, you must be totally aware. Now I want you to rewrite the character's backstory and be even more specific.

4. Describe the Character's Current Behavior

Take everything you have up to this point and determine what your character's behavior might exhibit at this moment. This will be your character's default. As the plot develops, they should also develop. The result is that they might act totally different to a certain situation by the end of your story.

5. Raise the Stakes

Emotions can be extreme so don't be afraid to raise the stakes. Push your characters to their limits when dealing with their desires and fears. It happens to all of us sometimes and nothing creates more dynamic characters than to show the audience how they will react under extreme situations. Look back on your own life and see how you reacted in extreme situations. Have you ever fallen behind on your bills and came close to losing everything? Have you ever totaled your favorite car? How did you react in these situations? Threaten your characters. When they triumph in the face of such adversity, your audience will love them even more.

6. Don't Meddle with your Characters

As the writer, your job is to observe and write down how your characters react during any given situation. If you have done all of the background stuff then your characters will not need any help from you. You have to just let them go and see what happens. Drop them into a scene and then use your imagination to see what they do next. Well written characters will make their own decisions. This is a difficult fact for some new writers to grasp but it is very true. Your only job is to document what they determine is the best course of action. I understand that this might all sound complicated right now but eventually (if you keep writing) it will finally hit you with the velocity of a semi truck.

7. Follow your Plot

Finally, just drop your characters into the plot and let them play. If you are being surprised by your characters' actions then you're on the right track. If you find yourself controlling them too much, you should develop them further.

6

Plotting the Way

By now you should have the overall idea of your story laid out. You should also have your characters ready to take on their roles. However, a story and plot are two entirely different things.

Your story's **main plot** revolves around a single idea and is dependant on a single outcome. Your protagonist will move from Act 1 to Act 2 and then finally to Act 3.

Subplots are scattered in between and usually involve other characters.

A plot involves a cause and effect. A story is just the string of events. In other words, your audience will be entertained by the story while your plot helps them put all of the pieces together. A plot is the glue that holds the story together and makes it believable.

There are hundreds of books out there that are devoted to different methods of developing plots. However, I will shoot straight with you. Those methods might have worked for those particular authors, but they might not work for you.

Screenwriting has a lot of rules that are set in stone, like formatting. You must follow formatting rules to the letter. However, when it comes to plotting you will need to find what works best for you. So don't try and follow some specific formula. Leave formulas to scientists and mathematicians. You're a writer so there is no *right* way to plot your script. Find something that works for you. It's all on your shoulders.

Let's take a look at some of the plotting details that you will need to consider. Think of this as a tool more than a formula. Feel free to modify it to meet your own goals.

Plot Outlining

Here is a simple checklist that you can follow in order to plot your screenplay. Each of these four important elements will be discussed in more detail.

1. What is your Genre? We actually discussed this in Chapter 3.

2. What's the main conflict of your story?

3. List the three main plot points in your story.

4. Develop an elevator pitch.

What's the main conflict in your story?

We have already discussed how a story should be laid out in a three act format. Each of these acts is developed through a number of sequences. Furthermore, we have discussed how your characters should be developed in a way that shapes your overall story. Your protagonist should be involved in some form of major conflict. What will this conflict be?

- Losing a job?
- Having an affair?
- Death?
- Murder?
- A fatal disease?

- Revenge?
- Treasures or riches?
- An adventure?
- Being framed for murder?
- Falling in love with the wrong person?
- A love triangle?
- Righting a wrong?
- Family issues?
- Sibling rivalry?
- A lost love?
- Betrayal?

Creating tension for your characters is not enough though. Your plot needs a deeper meaning. This is yet another reason that backstory is so important. Aren't you glad that you took the time to write all of that backstory?

Always consider the effect that the plot will have on a character – more importantly, how he/she will develop as a result.

- What will change your character? Define this turning point now.
- What steps will your protagonist have to go through in order to make it through this change?
- How will you test your character's resolve? Define how he/she will stay on course. They should fail in the beginning but each failure leads to a skill that will help them succeed the next time.
- What will he/she encounter along the way?
- What obstacles will get in your protagonist's way?

Consider some of the best movies and shows. Now define the moments when the protagonist was thrown into a situation where they were forced to confront their greatest fear. Now that you're watching television from a writer's perspective, you will start to notice things like this.

List the three main plot points in your story.

There are several major turning points throughout any movie. If you've been watching movies from a writer's perspective then you understand these moments. They typically reveal new information and lead into other events. After a turning point, the plot always takes on a new direction.

These events are the plot points. They go by many different names but the most commonly used ones follow this:

1. Inciting Incident

2. Plot Point I

3. Mid Point

4. Plot Point II

You should define these plot points before you even start writing. They give you a direction and serve to prevent writers from having to think too much when we should be writing. By now, you should know that's the theme of this book. Think as little as possible when writing. Everything should come from your imagination, not your logic.

The **Inciting Incident** happens within the first 10

pages of a screenplay. It is the incident that sets the whole story into motion.

Plot Point I generally happens between pages 20 and 30. It serves as the first major turning point.

The **Mid Point** takes place halfway through the screenplay and serves as the next major twist.

Plot Point II is the last one and happens around page 85-90. It is usually the final twist before the story's resolution.

Define these twists in your story now. Setting up the correct structure for your screenplay will help you write without having to stop and think. Plus it allows you to break up your story into manageable sections instead of tacking the whole thing at once.

Stop what you're doing and define those plot points now.

Once you have those plot points laid out, it's time to move onto developing your pitch. Yes, you read that correctly. Your pitch should be developed now.

Developing an Elevator Pitch

Later in the book, we will be discussing how you should pitch your screenplay to movies and producers. However, that type of pitch is much more elaborate than an elevator pitch.

Have you told anyone that you're planning to write a screenplay? If so, then I bet the first thing they asked was, "Really? What's it about?"

You're stumped and incoherently ramble about the essence of your story. Or worse, you say "I don't know how to describe it."

The reason is because our job is to write. We don't consider that we need to have a pitch ready just in case we are asked this question. True, we know our story inside and out. That's not the issue. The problem is that we don't know how to explain this in only a few seconds.

That's the job of an elevator pitch. It should describe your story in the time that it takes an elevator to get from one floor to the next. So you have 10-15 seconds.

Why this fast? Hollywood executives simply do not have time to listen to long, drawn out pitches. So you need to learn to present your idea succinctly, and quickly.

Creating your Elevator Pitch

The whole concept of trying to describe your story in just 10-15 seconds seems like an impossible feat. The bad news is that it's not an easy skill to master. The good news is that once you master it, you will be ahead of most other writers. I'm going to make this process as simple as humanly possible.

List each of the following on paper:

1. Your protagonist's external conflict.

2. Your protagonist's internal conflict.

3. Your protagonist's goals

4. Your protagonist's motivations.

5. The setting and genre of your screenplay.

Now take these five statements and try to craft them into two compelling sentences. Then say them aloud.

Time how long it takes you to complete them. Edit accordingly.

Once you have your elevator pitch, practice saying it. Start out in front of a mirror. Once you are happy with your pitch, start using it on your friends and gauge their reactions. Ask them the following questions:

- Does it make sense?
- Does it sound interesting?
- Is it something you would like to see?

Once you have their feedback, you can determine what works and what does not. If it needs to be fixed then by all means fix it. Once you have a working elevator pitch, you are better equipped to answer the question “what’s it about?”

Using Master Plots to Form your Story Arc

There are basic templates that all stories are formed around. Using one of these templates will make it much easier for you to plot your story. There’s no need to reinvent the wheel.

1. Quest: Most of you are familiar with movies like *'The Wizard of Oz'*. Quests are plots that are based around a central quest. The protagonist embarks on a quest to find something that will change their life. This can be a physical possession or even some form of life-changing wisdom. The main rule is that you need to tell your audience exactly what it is that your protagonist seeks and why they seek it.

2. Adventure: Adventures are often mistaken for quests but they are completely different themes. An adventure packs more action than a quest – which revolves more around a character's personal journey. *'The Lord of the Rings'* serves as a great example of an adventure plot. While it could easily be mistaken as a quest, the fact that the story focuses more on multiple characters and their struggle against dark forces makes it an adventure.

3. Pursuit: In this type of plot, one of the characters is being chased. Two prime example of a pursuit are *'The Terminator'* and *'The Fugitive'*.

4. Rescue: A rescue involves a three-way triangle between the protagonist, antagonist, and a victim. The plot follows as the protagonist tries to rescue the victim from the antagonist. This is one of the easier themes to plot.

5. Escape: In this theme, the protagonist is trying to escape from confinement. It could be prison or a deserted island. If your protagonist is trapped somewhere and they plan to escape, then chances are that your theme should be an escape. *'Shawshank Redemption'* is a perfect example of a movie that is built around an escape.

6. Revenge: This is also a very simple type of plot. As the name implies, the protagonist sets out to seek revenge on another character –often the antagonist.

7. Riddles: This theme focuses on events that the audience must evaluate and try to figure out. Mystery novels are all great examples of this theme. The reader is given clues and then the truth is revealed in the end.

8. Rivalry: At least two characters are competing for the same goal. In this type of plot, the protagonist and antagonist must be equally matched in the beginning.

9. Underdog: This type of plot works in the same way as the rivalry with one exception: the protagonist is at a huge disadvantage in the beginning. The protagonist will eventually gain the skills necessary to overcome those disadvantages.

10. Temptation: This plot shows a battle between ying and yang – temptation versus control. The protagonist struggles to deal with what is right and what is wrong. When your protagonist gives into the temptation, they will gain valuable experience.

11. Metamorphosis: This fun theme allows you to transform your character from one thing into another. The change is always physical. *''The Fly'* and *'Big'* are two great examples of metamorphosis.

12. Transformation: No, this does not refer to the movie 'Transformers' but rather a change in the protagonist's emotional or spiritual level. For example, if the protagonist switches places with their younger self then they are undergoing a transformation in order to gain a better understanding of themselves.

13. Maturation: In this theme, we have an older character who is still living an immature lifestyle. He/she cannot commit to anything. Something will have to happen that gets this character to grow up. The movie *'Hitch'* is a prime example of the maturation theme.

14. Love: Something will always get in the way of your protagonist's quest to find true love. There are a lot of different ways to approach a love story. Just remember that you need a protagonist, a love interest, and something standing between them and finding happiness.

15. Forbidden Love: This theme also revolves around love but the catch is that the protagonist pursues a love interest that they should not. 'Romeo and Juliet' is the most popular type of forbidden love story. A close second is 'City of Angels'.

16. Sacrifice: A sacrifice must come at a high cost and the protagonist must undergo a major change during the course of this type of story. They should start out at a moral low and work their way up. The audience must understand why this character is making the sacrifice or else it won't be believable.

17. Discovery: Self-discovery would be a more specific name for this theme but I'll use the same vernacular as the industry. A theme of discovery often embodies your protagonist trying to discover their own purpose in life. A series of events often propels this journey and focuses more on the character themselves rather than their actions.

18. Wretched Excess: This type of plot provides the audience with an opportunity to consider what could happen to them and how it would affect their lives. Greed can ultimately change a character's viewpoints – sometimes for the worse.

19. Ascension: This theme holds a moral dilemma that tests the protagonist. In ascension, they make the morally right choice.

20. Descension: This is like *Ascension* but with the opposite result. The protagonist will make the morally wrong choice.

Final Thought on Plot

Are you still scratching your head trying to determine a plot for your story? There's nothing more frustrating for a writer than to be awesome characters but no plot make them shine. If you're having problems then find a quiet place and listen carefully to your characters. Your protagonist should give you direction. If not, then you need to rebuild your protagonist. So make major changes to your character to mix it up.

Revamp your characters until a plot jumps out and slaps you across the face!

7

Act I: The Beginning

If you've made it this far then stop and give yourself a pat on the back. You have taken the hardest steps of writing – character development and determining a theme. Now it's time to actually lay out the full plot of your amazing story.

Every scene should be treated like its own short story. It should have a goal, attempt, and setback or achievement.

Ask yourself the following questions for every scene:

About Characters

- Which characters will be in the scene?
- How many characters will be in the scene?
- Does every character in the scene have a purpose? If not, then remove them.

- What are the characters' purpose in the scene?
- How will the characters react?

About the Scene

- What scenario will the characters in the scene be facing?
- Does the scene take the plot in a new direction?
- Is it day or night?
- What time of the day/night does the scene take place?

Location

- Where does the scene take place?

It all starts in Act I. You establish your protagonist and maybe even your antagonist. The very first scene will either make or break your screenplay. If you don't hook the audience right away then you will lose their interest.

When writing, it's important to remember that you will need to make a visual impact on your audience with every sentence. You are also setting them up for the scene that follows. Never, ever include a sentence that accomplishes nothing.

The opening image that you impose on your audience should summarize your entire screenplay. Include powerful metaphors. For example, depression can be symbolized through rain and gloom. A gunshot might symbolize heart pounding action. Sunshine symbolizes happiness. These are hidden ways that a writer can pour emotions into their audience's hearts without them even realizing it!

Now let's look at the three components of a scene. Every scene must follow this sequence.

The **goal** is what the main character in the scene is hoping to achieve. It's implied at the beginning of the scene.

After the goal is established, the character will then **attempt** to achieve the goal of the scene.

At the end of a scene, the character is **setback** in some form or another. The setback also sets up the next scene's goal, which is usually a direct response to this setback.

NOTE: A character can achieve his/her goal at the end of the scene. However, they must either achieve the goal or experience a setback.

Placing the Scene

When placing a scene, keep in mind that it must progress the story and that each scene involves some kind of conflict. A scene can serve many purposes.

1. A scene must always progress the story.

2. Scenes reveal the conflict of the plot.

3. A scene can be used to introduce a new character.

4. Scenes showcase a character's strengths and weaknesses. Usually one or the other is shown in different scenes. It's rare to include all in one scene.

5. Scenes can reveal secret information to the audience.

6. They set the mood using symbolism.

7. Every scene must enhance the story's theme.

If a scene does not serve a purpose, delete it!

In most cases, the opening scene throws the audience directly into the middle of the story. The idea is to grab your audience's attention right away. *'Indiana Jones'* movies always start with a breathtaking sequence of Indiana Jones on a treasure hunt of some kind.

The Writer versus The Director

This is an area where many new writers make directors angry. They try and do their job for them! A writer should tell a director what to shoot but never how to shoot it.

Including too many camera angles can really piss off a director. While it's okay to include them when absolutely necessary, they should be used sparingly – or in most cases, never at all. The Director uses his skills to transform your screenplay into a working script. They determine how an actor should act and how a cameraman should shoot the scene.

For example, it would be necessary to include a camera shot in your screenplay if there were a stain of blood on the wall that MUST be shown to the audience.

As the writer, you should focus more on the story than the exact movements, actions, and shots within a scene. Focus on location, dialogue, and description but never on stuff that the director should be doing.

Point of View (POV)

Every scene should be from a character's point of view so you should establish this immediately. This character then allows the audience to experience things the same way that they do. Most screenplays use a single POV throughout the entire script. Although using multiple POVs has been done before, you should probably stick to just one until you get a full grasp on screenwriting.

Modeling

We discussed modeling earlier when creating the characters used in your screenplay. Now let's expand on that strategy to include your screenplay's scenes. Modeling a scene means that you should take a scene that you already know from an experience in real life and then model it into your script.

When modeling, you can set your story in your hometown or even make up a fictional name for the setting but model it after your hometown. Scenes can also be either generic or specific.

Generic Scene = PARK

Specific Scene = CENTRAL PARK

It's always better to model specific scenes after something you know for real. This is why most writers base their earliest works on their hometown. It allows them to get very specific with details like store names, street names, popular locations, etc.

If you decide to model after your hometown then it's worth noting that you do not have to actually tell your audience the name of the town you're modeling. On the other hand, if you decide to write about a city that you know little about, then stick with generic settings.

Ending a Scene

The audience should be left wanting more at the end of every scene. A scene generally ends with its main character failing to achieve their goal. It sets up the following scene where the situation can either get worse or the plot takes a new direction.

Scenes can either end on a positive note or a negative note. This is known as the **polarity** of a scene. If you really want to keep your audience on their toes, always end a scene on the opposite polarity as you started it. For example, if the scene started out on a positive note, then end it on a negative one.

As soon as your characters seem to be doing well, throw a wrench into the mix to really mess with them! Stir the pot and make it get worse again. The opposite is also true. When things seem hopeless, give them a lucky break to get the ball rolling again.

Always end your scene as soon as possible. **DO NOT OVERWRITE!** Overwriting is the single most common mistake made by new screenwriters.

8

Act II: The Middles

Keeping the Tension

Act I is designed to introduce the audience to the main characters of the story. If you've done a good job up to this point then your audience will desperately want to know what happens next. So Act II should keep their interest.

I personally feel that Act II is the most important part of a screenplay. This is when most movies and books are either made or broken. You cannot afford to screw up here! Watch your favorite movie and pay close attention to how Act II develops. Any movie that is great has a perfectly written second act.

Keeping the tension high means that you will need to create new conflicts on top of your plot's main conflict.

Continue to raise the stakes. Now is the time to start utilizing that strong backstory that you spent so much time working on. Sprinkle hints in every scene but never give everything away all in one go.

You want the audience to always wonder, *'What happened to this person to make them act this way?'*

You can eventually tell them but wait until as late in the story as possible. People tend to find it much more interesting if they have to wonder *why* rather than knowing. It's like a magic trick. They seem amazing until you are shown how it's done. Then it's kinda lame.

An audience loves to make assumptions. This is one of the most fun aspects of being a writer. So let them assume and then completely blow their minds when you reveal the truth.

Finding the Conflict

Choose a random movie and watch it. Separate each Act and then find the conflicts in Act II. Make a list of each scene in Act II and then list the conflict for each scene.

Once you have this list, you can see what works and what doesn't. You can see how the writer formed the story.

Still Having Problems?

If you feel that your story is falling flat and seems uninteresting, then you should leave your desk and go out. The world is full of new experiences that might just inspire you. So go spend a day at the local café or go out to a restaurant and enjoy a meal. Take notes of what others are doing around you.

Just one conversation could inspire you to change something in your screenplay. Sometimes, all that's missing is one minor element.

9

Act III: Endings

Act III comes directly after the climax and serves to wrap up the story. First, let's look at the climax though since we have not gone over it yet.

Climax

The climax is what you've been building towards throughout your entire screenplay. In the movie Titanic, the climax was when the ship finally sunk into the depths of the ocean. Everyone knew it was coming. All of the tension in the movie built up to that moment.

A climax should make a viewer feel just as Titanic did – breathless and heart pounding. It's where the end truly begins. Your audience should be emotionally drained after viewing it. The audience will not be able to take anymore surprises after the climax. They only want to see what happens to their beloved characters. This is the moment when the writer really gets to talk to the audience. Act III is when we have their 100% undivided attention – so long as Acts I and II were compelling.

The Resolution

Your characters can now take in all that's happened to them throughout the story and put it together. They faced challenges around every turn that truly tested them. Now their development will be complete. They are not the same person they were in the beginning.

Your protagonist will have either succeeded or failed to achieve their overall goal. If they did fail, then that failure needs to still feel satisfactory.

Consider the movie *'Rocky'*. Rocky's goal was to win the title but in the end, he lost. However, he developed as a person and achieved a moral victory. So even though he failed to achieve his goal, the audience still feels satisfied since he achieved a huge moral victory.

Now consider the movie *'Gone with the Wind'*. The

audience waited for three full hours for Scarlett to finally make her decision. She finally got over Ashley but then we were thrown a huge twist. Rhett had enough and simply replied to her love with one of the most famous lines in cinema history, “Frankly my dear, I don’t give a damn.” Her change came too late and she was left reeling. What will happen to her in the future? We, as the audience, can only assume but we hope that the epiphany improves her life.

Exercise

Choose one of your favorite movies and define the climax, resolution, and ending. Consider how these all worked and what toll they took on you as a viewer. Then consider how it affects you as a screenwriter. Finally, rewrite your own ending for the movie.

10

Formatting your Screenplay

You've written that masterpiece. You're almost there so now would be a bad time to really screw up, wouldn't it? Well formatting is a common area where mistakes are made. You might have the best story in the world but if your screenplay is not formatted correctly, then no agent or producer is going to want to read it. Don't worry though. Follow these tips to ensure that your script is going to be read.

Size Does Matter

Rule of thumb states that every page of a screenplay is equivalent to one minute of screen time. This might not always be the case but it's the method used to estimate how long a movie will run. Since most movies are around 2 hours, then your screenplay should be around 120 pages right? Wrong!

Formatting your Screenplay

You should focus on getting your screenplay as close to 90 pages as possible. The reason is because agents do not like to read 120 page screenplays. If you can peak their interest in 90 pages, then they will help you build on it. However, do not send out a 120 page screenplay and then wonder why no one is reading it. So now let's trim up that screenplay.

The first thing to do is keep your scenes as short as possible. If a sentence does not add value to the scene, remove it. If a sentence can be removed without changing the scene, delete it.

Avoid camera angles like the plague. Remove any that are not 100% essential to your story. Other directions should be removed as well. Scenes should be used to convey your story, not show what is going to be seen on the big screen. Give the director just enough information to tell your story – nothing more and nothing less. Your essentials should be dialogue, locations, sounds, and some detail.

Formats and trends do change each year but so long as you get a grasp on the basics, you'll be just fine. You can purchase scripts for around $10 from various venues online. Read these to get a better understanding of how a script is formatted.

I recommend that you invest in a screenwriting program right away. They allow you to focus more on telling your story and less on format. They are absolutely necessary if you really want to be a screenwriter. The two best programs are Final Draft and Movie Magic Screenwriter.

The Title Page

How your title page looks is the first impression your screenplay is going to make on an agent or producer so you need to get it perfect. Follow these steps exactly:

1. Use Courier and Courier New fonts.

2. The title of your screenplay should be 25 lines from the top of the page.

3. Place 2 lines between the title and "Written by:" "Adapted by:" or "By".

4. Place your name and contact information in the bottom, right hand corner.

5. NEVER include images on the cover page.

You can view any professional screenplay to take note of the cover page. Remember, anything short of perfect will be seen as unprofessional.

Scene Formats

Scene headings should be margined 1.5 inches from the left edge of the paper and 1 inch from the right. Again, if you buy screenwriting software then you never have to worry about this.

Scene numbers are only included on 'shooting scripts" so you should not include these on your screenplay.

When a scene changes, a new heading must be added to the beginning of the next scene. Here's how a scene heading looks:

INT. HIDDEN ROOM UNDER TEMPLO MAYOR – DAY

It's divided into three sections.

INT. or EXT. determines whether the scene takes place indoors or outdoors. INT. means indoors – EXT. means outdoors.

Location is listed next. Describe the location in as much detail as needed for a director to set the scene. Be sure not to use any adjectives in the scene heading. For example, if I were to use "DARK, HIDDEN ROOM UNDER TEMPLO MAYOR" then it would not be correct.

Finally, the **time of day** is listed last. In most cases, DAY or NIGHT are good enough but you can be more specific if the story calls for it. MORNING, AFTERNOON, EVENING, SUNRISE, or SUNSET are all allowed but should be used only if the story calls for it.

When making note of a sound in a screenplay then it should be in ALL CAPS. If a character is making the sound (humming, etc.) then it does not need to be capitalized.

Dialogue should be centered and placed under the speaking character's name. The character's name should be in all capital letters. Again, if you buy screenwriting software then you never have to worry about this. Go buy it! Seriously. You will never be a professional screenwriter until you get the software.

Action in a Scene

The **action** of a scene is where you show the audience what is happening. It's always written in the present tense. It starts two lines below the scene heading. Always remember that this isn't a novel so you don't need to describe how a character feels. This comes across in your dialogue.

Action should be kept to an absolute minimum. Don't bog a reader down with huge scene that explains every move. Get across the necessary information and then move on. As a rule of thumb, keep action around four lines per scene. Also break it up into chunks of action rather than a huge mess.

Utilize action verbs that allow the reader to visualize the

scene. It should be brief, but powerful. Don't explain a scene or talk through the action.

When you use a character's name for the first time in a screenplay, then it should be placed in ALL CAPS.

If a character's dialogue is interrupted by an action sequence, then you must place ***(cont.)*** next to his/her name if they speak again before another character. If they are not on the screen, then use ***(O.S.)*** after their name. If they are being voiced over or are narrating, then use ***(V.O.)***.

Once more, I recommend that you purchase screenwriting software so you don't have to worry about this. I'm not pitching software here. I'm simply telling you that if you purchase it, you will not have to worry about these details. You'll be able to just write.

Transitions

Transitions are used with a film moves immediately from one scene to the next and this change is important to the screenplay. They should be placed on the right side (justified) of the page and are followed by a colon. Common transitions include:

CUT TO: This transitions directly to the next scene. Also, in most cases the scene following this transition omits the heading.

DISOLVE TO: This transition is used to gradually fade one scene into another. It generally indicates the passage of time.

INTERCUT WITH / INTERCUT BETWEEN: This indicates the start of a sequence of swapping back and forth between two scenes. All following scenes are labeled with BACK TO: to indicate that the scene is shifting.

It's recommended that you keep these to a bare minimum. Determine if it's essential to your story. If not, then let the director do his job and add these later.

11

How to Write a Screenplay in 60 Days

So now that you have an understanding of the basics of screenwriting, you can start working towards your overall goal. At the beginning of this book you signed a contract so you are now faced with the task at hand. Don't be scared though. You're now equipped with a much better understanding of how to make this all easier. Don't give up now when you're so close.

Writing a screenplay in 60 days is not as daunting a task as you might think. It's completely doable. Your draft should take up most of that time, leaving a couple of weeks for revisions. Trust me, writing the draft is not that difficult so long as you just write.

Be prepared to experience some annoying discomfort from time-to-time. If it were easy then everyone would do it. Keep writing even when words seem hard. You can fix it later so just write.

On the other hand, you will get into what us writers call ***The Writer's Zone***. During this time, it's extremely important to avoid distractions. These are the times when your best writing will occur. It's completely random and easy to get pulled out of.

Whether it's an easy or difficult time, just keep writing. Creativity is a wondrous thing. The preparation that goes with creation is not so wondrous. It can be downright annoying!

Beating Writer's Block

We've all heard of this powerful curse. It's cursed on all four corners of the Earth. Now I'm going to reveal something that might be considered very controversial.

Writer's block is a myth.

You read that correctly. There is no magical curse out there that just suddenly prevents you from writing. It happens when we try and edit our work while we write. We're so close to our story that we need it to be perfect.

So one word causes us to stop writing to try and get it perfect. This should be taken care of during the revision phase, not when writing a draft.

Avoid writer's block by sitting down and writing. It's that simple. Worry about editing later. Sure, sometimes you're going to write absolute trash. That's okay. You can fix it later. Once the words start to flow, your quality will improve.

Ignoring your inner editor will save you so many headaches. As humans, we tend to overcomplicate tasks that should be simple. Writing is no exception. So tell that editor in your head to get the heck out! His job comes later. Again, just sit down and write. Now let's work out a schedule that should help you meet your goal of a screenplay every 60 days.

Week 1: Develop your characters and their backstory. Spend an entire week writing about each of your characters. Use the tips in this book to bring your characters to life.

Week 2: Week 1 should focus on character development so now we will devote a whole week to developing the plot. Start out by laying out your plot points. Then focus on everything in between. A week should be more than enough time to plan your plot perfectly.

Week 3-5: Start writing now. Your goal should be 5 pages a day. If you write 5 pages per day for 21 days, that is 105 pages. Since you only need 90, you have some wiggle room. You should not feel rushed and 5 pages a day is an easy goal to achieve.

Week 6+7: These two weeks are dedicated to revising your screenplay. At this point, you can bring back that inner editor. No one gets it right the first time. Revisions are always a must so be sure that you follow through with this step. Don't be afraid to rewrite an entire scene if it doesn't work. Try and get the first batch of revisions done within 10 days.

Then put your screenplay to the side for at least 4 days before moving on to the next phase.

Week 8: Go through your screenplay from a fresh perspective and get it into perfect shape. Ensure that it is not longer than 90 pages.

You should feel accomplished if you make it this far because you have achieved something that 99% of people don't. You have written a complete screenplay!

Finding the Time to Write

Five pages a day is not a difficult goal to achieve but sometimes it can be difficult to find the time to actually sit down and get it done. My advice is to schedule the time right now. If you have to wake up an hour earlier than normal, then do it. If you are watching television for 2-3 hours each night then cut into that time. Do whatever it takes to actually sit down and start writing. You only need 1 hour a day to meet your goal of 5 pages.

Finding a Place to Write

Choosing the perfect place to write is just as important as any other strategy that we have mentioned in this book. A common mistake is that some people try and write with children screaming in the background or dogs barking in the street when they are annoyed by noise.

On the other hand, complete silence might be a distraction. It's really a personal preference but you need to eliminate any distractions. There are some decisions that are mandatory though. They are as follows:

- Turn off your cell phone
- Close out your email
- Stay off the internet
- Tell friends and family not to disturb you during this time

You will want a clutter free work area. Easy access to things like your notes, journal, references, and dictionary should all be within reach. Decorate your writing area with inspirational objects like motivational posters and books that inspire you.

Plot Block

Unlike my controversial belief of writer's block being a myth, plot block is not a myth. However, it only happens when you have not prepared enough. If you spent the first two weeks laying out your characters and plot, then you will not be faced with this problem.

It's worth noting that you should never set your characters in stone. Allow them to develop on their own and if something changes, then go with the flow. You're just observing them.

Using the Correct Tone

So many writers out there believe that they must change their voice in order to write. This is the last thing they should be doing! Never try and sound like someone else. Write from the heart. Use your own voice. You'll do just fine, trust me.

Write for yourself, not for an audience.

Enter your Screenplay into Contests

This can be for two reasons. First, it sets a deadline for you to complete your screenplay which is a huge source of motivation. Second, it gives you a way to assess how good your screenplay holds up against competition. Both are extremely helpful.

Just be careful when entering screenplay contests since some are not worth it. In fact, some are outright scams. You want to search for the ones that industry specialists use to hunt for new talent. That way you have a change to catch someone's eye if your screenplay stands out.

Learning to Take Criticism

Here's where I'm going to lose a lot of readers but I'm not going to beat around the bush. You're going to get rejected. You're going to get told that your screenplay flat out sucks. Having put so much time and energy into your screenplay, it's going to hurt when you hear this. You will need to grow a thick skin if you want to be successful in Hollywood. Use this type of criticism as a tool. Don't let it stop you from writing.

The trick is to find someone to give you the kick you need. Friends and family are often a good first choice but sometimes they lack the callous to give you the criticism you need. It's better to get an honest opinion (especially when it's bad) than to have someone tell you what they believe you want to hear.

Ask anyone who reads your screenplay the following questions:

1. Was the story easy to follow?

2. Are the characters believable?

3. How did the dialogue sound in your head? Did it seem like a real conversation?

4. Did the action make you feel like you were right there?

5. Did the plot grab you from the beginning and pull

you all the way through until the end?

6. Were there any parts that seemed boring?

7. Did any of the plot leave you guessing or was it hard to understand?

Once you get honest feedback, do not let it offend you. You asked for honesty and that's what you got. We all have an opinion.

Take constructive criticism professionally. Look into the issues and either fix them or move on. Just because an individual doesn't like a movie, that doesn't always mean that it was a bad movie. If your screenplay has real issues then you need to know. One scene could be holding your entire screenplay from its full potential.

If multiple people are telling you that there's a problem with the same scene, then chances are that you should rewrite it. They probably have a valid point.

Remember that your first screenplay isn't likely going to break you into the industry. No amount of rewriting can change that. It's more of a learning experience in the beginning. Once you have done your absolute best, then move on to the next screenplay. You will only get better and once you gain experience, you can pull that old screenplay out of the drawer and tweak it.

Take a Break

Creativity is a fuel that writers use to power their storytelling skills. Sometimes the tank will simply run empty. When that happens, you have to take a break from writing. Take a few days off. Enjoy the world around you. Do you like golfing? Then golf for a few days until your creativity recharges.

12

Get your Screenplay Read

You've put in a lot of effort to make it this far. I wish I could tell you that all of your hard work is over now, but it's not. You have to get your script read by an agent. That brings me to a huge tip that you should always keep in mind.

You must find an agent FIRST. Producers rarely look at unsolicited screenplays.

I'll probably mention that a few more times before the end of this book. It's that important. Anyway, let's get going.

Being a successful screenwriter is so much more than merely writing the next award wining screenplay. It takes a lot of knowledge to become successful in Hollywood. Don't let that scare you though. You'll get there. Everyone has to start somewhere. Just start marketing and you'll gain valuable experience.

Here are a couple of easy tips on how you should get started:

- First and foremost, you need a list of agents to send query letters to. So I recommend that you go out and buy the *Hollywood Creative Directory*. It includes a comprehensive list of agents and how to contact them. It will become your best friend. *The Writer's Market* is another great book to invest in.
- Bookmark The Writer's Guild website and read through some of the powerful information provided. It will teach you valuable lessons and motivate you.

How to Approach Agents

A query letter is your best approach here. I'll devote a whole section to writing the perfect query letter but for now, know that it should always be your initial approach. I'll go ahead and give you a few tips. You should write these down and post them.

Keep it as short and to the point as possible. Agents are constantly sent query letters so they are not going to take the time to read long ones. Your logline will serve to hook them.

A perfect logline is the best way to improve your odds of getting signed.

You can also increase your odds by taking the time to address your letter to the individual who will be reading it. Every listing includes a phone number so call and ask. Explain to them why they are a good match for your screenplay. Agents love to be pitched to personally. If you come across as generic, then your letter is not likely to impress them.

Try emailing them first since it's free. In today's world, email is starting to replace snail mail as the preferred method of getting query letters. Still, be sure to call and get the name of the individual who you will be emailing.

Always end all conversations with a polite "thank you". Never, under any circumstances, should you be rude. I don't care what kind of response you get. Say "thank you" and move on. You don't know how a rude reaction will haunt you in the future. Plus, as writers we need to stay positive. Being rude is just a bad idea.

Exercise in Industry Knowledge

I want you to open up that notebook of yours and make a list of what you know about Hollywood. Then make a list of what you don't know. Once you have both lists, ask yourself two questions:

1. What should you know that you do not know at this time?

2. How will learning this help me as a screenwriter?

Finding an Agent

As I stated earlier, you must find an agent before you approach producers. The reasons why producers will not look at unsolicited screenplays are purely legal. Many writers have thought they were due payment since they had the same idea for a movie that has been released. It may or may not have been true but not reading an unsolicited screenplay is their only method to completely eliminate the risk of being sued.

An agent will work tirelessly to get your screenplay out there. Their entire livelihood depends on them selling their clients' scripts to producers. They will have a vast Hollywood network. Agents should have forged relationships all throughout the industry so they are much better equipped to set up meetings with people who are more likely to actually listen to your pitch. Agents shop around to find the best fit for your screenplay.

Agents are going to be on the look for scripts that are in the highest demand. This demand changes from time-to-time so you should do your homework.

Here are some things that you should keep in mind when looking for an agent:

- First and foremost, learn what the agent's fees are. Understand what percentage of royalties they will get from your screenplay when it sells. The average is around 10%. Some agencies try and charge faxing fees, couriers, and other miscellaneous fees. Avoid these agents. You want an agent who depends on your screenplay being sold in order to make money. You do not want an agent who makes money simply by charging for faxes and other miscellaneous fees.

- Do your homework and research the agent. Find out how many clients they take on in a certain time period. Do they take on new writers? Visit their website or call them to answer any questions you might have.
- Address your query letter to the individual who will be reading it. Again, you can get this information from the directory or by calling the agent. Calling is often the best choice since it gives you an opportunity (sometimes) to give the agent your elevator pitch. Be enthusiastic when given the opportunity.
- Never submit a screenplay unless the agent asks for it.
- "Fortune is in the follow-up." That's one of my

favorite business quotes and it's so true. When an agent asks to see your screenplay, follow-up immediately! When sending out query letters, be sure to follow up with another. Explain in your initial letter that you will be following up and tell them when. Then be sure to actually follow through!

- Finding an agent is a difficult task but one that must not be skipped. Increase your dismal odds (yes, your odds are very bad) by doing everything in your power. Present your pitch professionally.
- Be sure that the agent you are pitching to understands the industry. They should live on the West coast and have experience in the business. They should also have a website that explains their agency.

Writing your Query Letter

Writing a letter that pitches your screenplay to agents is much more difficult than writing the screenplay itself. It's definitely an area that takes a lot of practice. It is also the most important part of your writing career. A query letter will either get your foot in the door or it will get the door slammed in your face.

Let's face it. Most agents will not want to read a 90 page screenplay from a nobody. Your query letter has to convince them that they should do just that. It should hook, subdue, and then give them a call to action. That call to action is to contact you and request the screenplay.

A query letter also gives you the opportunity to prove that you are a good writer. It will be the first impression that you make on an agent so make it a lasting one.

- Proofread the letter three times before sending it. Make sure there are absolutely no grammar or spelling mistakes.
- Address it to the appropriate person.
- Hook them with the first sentence.
- Include no more than two sentences about you. The rest should cover your screenplay.

- Include a call to action in the final sentence. Ask them the all important question: "Can I send you my script?"

Coping with Rejection

It's going to happen. You're going to get rejected more often that not. Almost any agent you submit a query to is going to reject your proposal. This isn't meant to scare you but it's simply a fact of life as a screenwriter. If you do your homework and know how agents tick, what they are looking for, and what's in demand then you will increase your chances significantly. Never take rejection personally. It will help you develop as a screenwriter. Use rejection letters to motivate you. Heck, I frame my favorite ones so that I can let them fuel me on a daily basis.

Don't be afraid to ask for critical feedback either. Most agents will not oblige but if they do, take their advice to heart. Use this knowledge to make improvements and make sure that you don't get defensive. Thank them and move on. Never argue. Arguing with a professional makes you look like an idiot. They know a lot more about the business than you do!

An honest critique is important for a number of reasons including:

- It gives you an outsider's perspective about plot holes, character development, and even dialogue.
- Maybe you missed something? Now you know.
- Hearing the words "it's not good enough" can motivate you to dedicating more time to perfecting it.

Just remember that even best-selling writers had to cope with rejection. J.K. Rowling (author of 'Harry Potter') was famously told that kids would never read her books.

Pitching your Screenplay

If you are lucky enough to get the attention of an agent or even signed by one, then they will shop around for a producer. So you will need to be prepared to pitch your screenplay to them when given the opportunity.

Agents will only set up these meetings; it's your job to actually pitch your idea. This is your chance to describe your story in full detail. Use anything that will bring it to life for the producer. If your screenplay is based on a true story, then try to have that person with you when you pitch it.

Be prepared. Know your story inside and out. Practice pitching in front of a mirror. Determine the selling point of your screenplay and be enthusiastic about it! Remember that when you're pitching, less is more.

If the producer likes your concept, then they are going to offer you an option. An option entails:

- A producer begins their search for financial backing and talent.
- An option states payment that a writer receives if the screenplay goes into production.
- An option also states if a writer will be required to make any revisions or if others will be hired to help with these revisions.
- It details if a writer will receive credit.

13

Giving yourself the Best Chance of Success

We have already discussed:

- The importance of understanding Hollywood
- How to develop an elevator pitch
- Why contests are important
- Writing a query letter
- Working with an agent
- How to pitch to producers
- Options and how they work

Right now, I recommend that you give your screenplay one more proofing. I know you're tired of reading the same script and want to move onto the next but it's so important that it contains no errors that I want you to give it one more read through. In fact, proofreading is an area where many people have problems so here are some options on how to get your screenplay perfect.

- Hire a professional editor. This costs money but is simply your best option to get it perfect. You can find professional freelancers who will not charge you an arm and a leg to proof your script.
- If you don't have the money to hire a professional, then consider getting a second part-time job to fund it.
- Don't get in a hurry. It's better to take the extra time to perfect your screenplay rather than rush one out that is filled with errors. In fact, I'd recommend that you start your next screenplay while letting the current one sit for a week or two. Then go back and proofread it a final time from a fresh perspective.

The Most Common Mistakes Found by Experts

The most common mistakes that are found by experts are:

- Poor writing quality
- Screenplay has no hook
- Unbelievable characters
- Story line that moves too slowly
- Not following the standard three act structure
- Not enough conflict
- Dialogue that sounds like it's coming from the writer and not characters
- Spelling, grammar, and formatting error

Made in the USA
Monee, IL
20 February 2021

60983139R00085